"The initial statement of the Hannover Principles ten years ago came like a breath of fresh air into the divisive world of environmental politics, helping people everywhere to rise above the tumult and finger pointing and get down to the real work: reinventing the artifacts that propel economic activity and, as importantly, rediscovering our sense of connection to one another and to life."

PETER SENGE
Senior Lecturer, Sloan School of Management

7. **Rely on natural energy flows.** Human designs should, like the living world, derive their creative force from perpetual solar income. Incorporate this energy efficiently and safely for responsible use.

8. **Understand the limitations of design.** No human creation lasts forever, and design does not solve all problems. Those who create and plan should practice humility in the face of nature. Treat nature as a model and mentor, not as an inconvenience to be evaded or controlled.

9. **Seek constant improvement by the sharing of knowledge.** Encourage direct and open communication between colleagues, patrons, manufacturers and users to link long-term sustainable considerations with ethical responsibility and to reestablish the integral relationship between natural processes and human activity.

The Hannover Principles should be seen as a living document committed to transformation and growth in the understanding of our interdependence with nature so that they may be adapted as our knowledge of the world evolves.

"Reading *The Hannover Principles* for the first time was an epiphany. This humane and eloquent epistle shows us how to imagine a new model for business and for life—a model that celebrates fairness, creativity and interdependence. It imagines a world where the desires of a few do not supersede the needs and wants of the many. It offers a blueprint for making intelligent and generous decisions. It astonished me with its clarity and power."

SUSAN LYONS
Susan Lyons Design

❧ ❧ ❧

"Ford Motor Company is transforming its historic Rouge manufacturing site into an icon of 21st century sustainable manufacturing. We have restored acres of native habitat, installed the world's largest green roof, renewed industrial architecture, demonstrated ground-breaking phytoremediation, revived natural day-lighting in our new assembly plant, and met or exceeded our standard financial criteria. The Hannover Principles have been a guiding light on this journey."

TIM O'BRIEN
Vice President, Corporate Relations
Ford Motor Company

The Hannover Principles
Design for Sustainability

William McDonough *&* Michael Braungart

10th ANNIVERSARY EDITION
With an Introduction by Teresa Heinz

The Hannover Principles

TENTH ANNIVERSARY EDITION

Copyright © 2003 by William McDonough + Partners and McDonough Braungart Design Chemistry. All rights reserved.

William McDonough + Partners
tel 434 979 1111
fax 434 979 1112
www.mcdonoughpartners.com

McDonough Braungart Design Chemistry
tel 434 295 1111
fax 434 295 1500
www.mbdc.com

ISBN 1-55963-635-1

Book design by Peter Massarelli

Printed in the United States of America

5 4 3 2 1

The text and cover of this book are printed with soy-based inks on 100% post-consumer recycled, processed chlorine-free paper.

The Hannover Principles was originally prepared for the City of Hannover, Germany, for EXPO 2000 by:

- William McDonough and Michael Braungart
- William McDonough Architects (New York, New York)
- The Environmental Protection Encouragement Agency (Hamburg, Germany)

This special edition is a revised and updated version of the original document issued by the City of Hannover in 1992.

The 10th anniversary edition of *The Hannover Principles* is a revised, updated version of the original, which was published in 1992. The first edition, commissioned by the City of Hannover, Germany, was conceived as a guide to the design of the 2000 World's Fair and some of its content was specifically addressed to designers who would be developing the fair site or participating in a design competition. No longer of pressing importance today, most of the references to the EXPO 2000 competition were not included in this edition. The Principles themselves, however, are still informing the ever-evolving conversation on design for sustainability, as is much of the background material included in the 1992 edition. By revising the original text and adding several new essays to this tenth anniversary edition, we hope both to invite readers "back to the well" and to put *The Hannover Principles* in perspective.

The new material includes an introduction by Teresa Heinz, an essay by William McDonough and Michael Braungart, and an afterword by David Rothenberg. Remaining from the first edition are the Principles, a section on the foundations of ecological design, and a substantial essay on the meaning of sustainability. The essay has been compressed and revised, but in the interest of maintaining historical integrity, its point of view remains the early 1990s. Its language, therefore, sometimes reflects that period's urgent use of "shoulds" and "musts" rather than the more celebratory language we use today, language that expresses our growing faith in humanity's ability to create, by design, mutually beneficial relationships between people and the natural world.

The Principles have not been revised. Though they, too, had an urgent birth and have the language to show for it, their value to us is timeless. Grounded in the enduring laws of nature, the Principles continue to be the source and standard for our designs.

In the original edition, the Oberstadtdirektor of the City of Hannover, Jobst Fiedler, wrote that the Principles were one of the 2000 World's Fair's "first exhibits: a sign of hope, a gesture of goodwill and an invitation to all everywhere to celebrate a new millennium with a fresh and positive perspective." We offer the tenth anniversary edition of *The Hannover Principles* in the same hopeful spirit.

CHRIS REITER
March 2003

CONTENTS

INTRODUCTION

I first became aware of William McDonough's work in 1984, when he redesigned the national headquarters of the Environmental Defense Fund. The redesign of the EDF office was a watershed event. Not only was it the first "green" office in New York City, it also laid the foundation for a new design philosophy: a commercially productive, socially beneficial and ecologically intelligent approach to the making of things that Bill and his colleague Michael Braungart would come to call eco-effectiveness.

When I hired Bill to design the Heinz family offices and Heinz Foundation offices in Pittsburgh in 1991, he and Michael had just been commissioned by the City of Hannover to develop a set of design principles for the 2000 World's Fair. Having chosen "Humanity, Nature and Technology" as the theme of the fair, the city wanted to showcase hopeful visions for a sustainable future. The Hannover Principles were to put forth an inspiring standard, presenting to the world the first coherent framework for rethinking design through the lens of sustainability.

Getting to know Bill and Michael as colleagues and friends over the last ten years has given me the opportunity to see firsthand the impact of the Hannover Principles. From their elegant insistence on "the rights of humanity and nature to co-exist" to their call to "eliminate the concept of waste," the Principles echo the deep human instinct—and wisdom—to care for the world. Indeed, they have become a cultural touchstone, providing information and grounding not just for the design community but also for all those devoted to bringing forth a world of social equity, environmental health and peaceful prosperity.

At their core is a simple truth: Human health, the strength of our economy and the well-being of our environment are all connected. I learned this lesson early in life, as a child growing up in Mozambique. In the East Africa of my youth, the interplay of nature, health and survival was a given, something that people who lived close to the natural world intuitively understood. For me, that understanding was reinforced by having a father who was a doctor. Observing him and the questions he asked of his patients taught me how illness can be related to environment and the practices of daily life.

We lived in a place where nature's laws of cause and effect were fairly clear. If you went swimming at sunrise or sunset, feeding time for sharks and river crocodiles (and indeed, for all the animals in the savannah), you might get a nasty nibble. We learned to respect the rules of the natural world because they had such obvious implications for people's personal well-being. Nature taught us the virtues of prevention—of solving problems by not creating them in the first place.

Industrialized societies tend to be less in touch with nature's rules. In the nineteenth century, the paradigm was that we should tame nature; in the twentieth, it became a sense that we are almost immune to its rules. Today, we tend to think of the natural world as somehow separate, an entity "out there" that can be controlled, held at bay or even ignored. Even our efforts to protect the environment have been informed by this "us versus it" mentality, a sense that we are in competition with the natural world and that the best we can hope for is to mitigate the damage we cause.

The simple genius behind the nine Hannover Principles was that they reframed the issue. Rather than take a certain amount of ecological harm as a given, with people on various sides of the environmental debate reduced to arguing over the permissible amount, Bill and Michael invited us to consider an alternative. Why not just design products and institutions that *support* the environment, they asked?

The Hannover Principles were the first expression of that transforming idea. In nine lean declarations they set forth a value system and a design framework that Bill and Michael continue to use as the foundation of their evolving design paradigm. As they write in *Cradle to Cradle: Remaking the Way We Make Things*, nature's cycles are not just lean and efficient; they are abundant, effective and regenerative. By going beyond mere efficiency to celebrate the abundance of nature, the practice of eco-effective, cradle-to-cradle design allows us to create materials, dwellings, workplaces, and commercial enterprises that generate not fewer negative impacts but more productivity, more pleasure and more restorative effects.

The key insight of eco-effective or cradle-to-cradle thinking is recognizing the materials of our daily lives—even highly technical, synthetic industrial materials—as *nutrients* that can be designed to circulate in human systems very much like nitrogen, water, and simple sugars circulate in nature's nutrient cycles. Rather than using materials once and sending them to the landfill—our current cradle-to-grave system—cradle-to-cradle materials are designed to be returned safely to the soil or to flow back to industry to be used again and again.

Far more than a theoretical notion, this central principle of sustainability can be readily seen in the work of Bill's architectural firm, William McDonough + Partners, and Bill and Michael's industrial design consultancy, McDonough Braungart Design Chemistry. Working with clients ranging from small companies like the Swiss textile mill Rohner to global megacorporations like the Ford Motor Company, both firms are showing that designers attuned to this cradle-to-cradle philosophy can replicate nature's closed-loop systems in the worlds of commerce and community. The result: safe, beneficial materials that either naturally biodegrade or provide high-quality resources for the next generation of products; buildings designed to produce more energy than they consume; cities and towns tapped into local energy flows; places in every human realm that renew a sense of participation in the landscape.

My own hopes for the urban landscapes of Pittsburgh brought *The Hannover Principles* home, literally. At the Earth Summit in Rio in 1992, where the Principles were introduced to the international community, I invited Bill and Michael to come to Pittsburgh to share their ideas. Both were invited to lecture at Carnegie Mellon University and, as I had hoped, the Hannover Principles became a part of the dialogue going on in Pittsburgh at the time about the region's environmental future.

Today, Pittsburgh is gaining national recognition as a leader in green building and sustainable design. In many ways, that began with the building of the Heinz family offices, which represented the first, commercial-scale use of sustainably harvested tropical wood. Our offices served as a laboratory and model for others to learn from, and not just locally. The Discovery Channel covered it; architectural magazines wrote about it; and builders, designers and architects from across the country came to study its features. Since then, the ideas articulated in the Hannover Principles have never been far from the minds of the staff at The Heinz Endowments as they have advanced our green building agenda in Pittsburgh over the past decade.

Those ideas are making communities from Pittsburgh to Chicago and from Shanghai to Barcelona better places to live. They are helping people create buildings and landscapes where natural processes unfold with renewed vitality. They are transforming product design and shaping the work of such influential companies and institutions as Ford, Nike, BASF, the University of California, the Woods Hole Research Center and Oberlin College. As more and more companies and institutions adopt these sustaining principles, there is also the chance that the global economy as a whole will begin to find robust health and long-term strength through the practice of intelligent design.

Ultimately, that is the enduring value of *The Hannover Principles* and the reason why this tenth anniversary edition is as fresh and necessary as ever. The Principles urge us to start seeing ourselves as part of the natural world and to replicate the joyful, productive and intelligent practice of life itself.

TERESA HEINZ
Washington, D.C.
March 2003

The
Hannover
Principles

➤

1. **Insist on the right of humanity and nature to co-exist** in a healthy, supportive, diverse and sustainable condition.

2. **Recognize interdependence.** The elements of human design interact with and depend upon the natural world, with broad and diverse implications at every scale. Expand design considerations to recognize even distant effects.

3. **Respect relationships between spirit and matter.** Consider all aspects of human settlement, including community, dwelling, industry and trade, in terms of existing and evolving connections between spiritual and material consciousness.

4. **Accept responsibility for the consequences of design** decisions upon human well-being, the viability of natural systems and their right to co-exist.

5. **Create safe objects of long-term value.** Do not burden future generations with requirements for maintenance or vigilant administration of potential dangers due to the careless creation of products, processes or standards.

6. **Eliminate the concept of waste.** Evaluate and optimize the full life cycle of products and processes to approach the state of natural systems, in which there is no waste.

7. **Rely on natural energy flows.** Human designs should, like the living world, derive their creative force from perpetual solar income. Incorporate this energy efficiently and safely for responsible use.

8. **Understand the limitations of design.** No human creation lasts forever, and design does not solve all problems. Those who create and plan should practice humility in the face of nature. Treat nature as a model and mentor, not as an inconvenience to be evaded or controlled.

9. **Seek constant improvement by the sharing of knowledge.** Encourage direct and open communication between colleagues, patrons, manufacturers and users to link long-term sustainable considerations with ethical responsibility and to reestablish the integral relationship between natural processes and human activity.

The Hannover Principles should be seen as a living document committed to transformation and growth in the understanding of our interdependence with nature so that they may be adapted as our knowledge of the world evolves.

THE HANNOVER PRINCIPLES AT TEN
William McDonough & Michael Braungart

A decade ago, when William McDonough Architects and the Environmental Protection Encouragement Agency (EPEA) developed the Hannover Principles for the 2000 World's Fair, design for sustainability was in its infancy. While the desire to move toward a solar-powered world had gained significant momentum among the environmentally conscious by 1992, and the ideas that inform ecological design had begun to manifest themselves in encouraging innovations in "green" architecture and technology, a coherent framework for applying sustainable design to *all* sectors of society had yet to emerge. The Hannover Principles were conceived as the first iteration of this new paradigm.

We knew at the time that our efforts were just a first step. Though we were striving to identify universal principles based on the enduring laws of nature, we also understood that our knowledge of the world was incomplete. So, too, was our ability to predict all the many ways in which the creativity of the world's designers, architects, business leaders, and NGOs would push design for sustainability beyond the limits we could imagine in 1992. Thus, we saw the Principles as a living document — a set of enduring ideals *and* an open system of thought that would evolve as it was put into practice.

And evolve it has. William McDonough + Partners (WM+P), McDonough Braungart Design Chemistry (MBDC), and EPEA continue to use and publish the Principles in their original form. Yet, as each firm applies the Principles in the design process or uses them to guide everyday decision-making, new ideas and practices emerge. The result: The Principles remain an enduring touchstone, their rigor drives innovation, and our design paradigm continues to mature.

This process, whether it plays out in a matter of weeks or over the course of years, begets enormous creativity. The generative power of Principle six provides a good example. Principle six says *Eliminate the concept of waste*. In 1992 this was a radical new concept. Designers and engineers were typically focused on reducing waste, on trying to be "less bad." The conventional wisdom held that using less energy and fewer materials and limiting the amount of toxic chemicals released into the air, water, and soil would guarantee a sustainable world. But Principle six demands something entirely different. Rather than attempting to mitigate the destructive effects of architecture and industry, eliminating the concept of waste demands that we begin to see our designs in a wholly positive light.

Pursuing that goal over the past decade has driven the evolution of an entirely new approach to design. When one takes seriously the idea that the concept of waste can be eliminated in the worlds of architecture, commerce, manufacturing, and transportation—indeed, in every sector of society—the purview of design shifts radically. Not only are we obliged to include the entire material world in our design considerations, we are asked to imagine materials in a whole new way. In today's world of trying to be "less bad," materials typically follow a one-way path to the landfill and waste managers intervene here and there to slow down the trip from cradle to grave. But when we are no longer content with simply managing waste, we can begin to create and use materials within *cradle-to-cradle* systems, in which there is no waste at all.

Rather than seeing materials as a waste management problem, cradle-to-cradle thinking sees materials as *nutrients* that cycle through either the *biological metabolism* or the *technical metabolism*. In the biological metabolism, the nutrients that support life on Earth—water, oxygen, nitrogen, carbon dioxide — flow perpetually through biological cycles of growth, decay and rebirth. There are no waste-management problems. Instead, waste equals food. The technical metabolism is designed to mirror natural nutrient cycles; it's a closed-loop system in which valuable, high-tech synthetics and mineral resources circulate in an endless cycle of production, recovery and reuse.

By specifying safe, healthful ingredients, designers and architects can create and use materials within these cradle-to-cradle cycles. Materials designed as *biological nutrients*, such as textiles for draperies, wall coverings and upholstery fabrics, can be designed to biodegrade safely and restore the soil after use, providing more positive effects, not fewer negative ones. Materials designed as *technical nutrients*, such as infinitely recyclable nylon carpet fiber, can provide high-quality, high-tech ingredients for generation after generation of synthetic products—again, a harvest of value. And buildings constructed with these nutritious materials and designed to "fit" within local energy flows articulate and enhance the connection between people and nature. Already well established through the work of WM+P, MBDC, and EPEA, cradle-to-cradle thinking represents a radical, ongoing revolution in design. Its source and sustenance: The laws of nature adapted to human design in the Hannover Principles.

When the Principles become practices, when industrial and architectural systems are modeled on the earth's flows of energy and nutrients, the notion that humanity must limit its ecological footprint is turned on its head. Indeed, as cradle-to-cradle thinking continues to be enriched by the inspired work of our colleagues at WM+P, MBDC and EPEA, we are increasingly able to design products and places that support life, that create footprints to delight in rather than lament. This changes the entire context of the design process. Instead of asking, "How do I meet today's environmental standards?" designers at WM+P, MBDC and EPEA are asking, "How might I create more habitat, more health, more clean water, more prosperity, more delight?"

Questions such as these, emerging from the daily application of the Hannover Principles, are stimulating the worldwide evolution of cradle-to-cradle design. They are driving "The Cradle-to-Cradle Revolution," a growing movement in which designers are developing safe materials, products, supply chains and manufacturing processes that allow us to celebrate human creativity and the world's natural abundance. In fact, just one year after the publication of the original edition of *The Hannover Principles*, we had the opportunity to develop a cradle-to-cradle upholstery fabric, Climatex Lifecycle, which is produced with completely safe ingredients and biodegrades after use. The design and production of Climatex Lifecycle, which launched a partnership between EPEA and MBDC and transformed a factory burdened with toxic wastes into one with only positive emissions, signaled the real-world efficacy of "waste equals food."

Just so, the Hannover Principles and cradle-to-cradle thinking are moving nations as vast and influential as China to begin to apply the intelligence of natural systems to their development plans. They are guiding the design of community plans that connect people to nature and to each other. They are inspiring the design of buildings like trees, which harvest the energy of the sun, sequester carbon, make oxygen, distill water and provide habitat for thousands of species.

And more. Imagine everything we do or make as a gesture that supports life, inspires delight and expresses intelligence in harmony with nature. Imagine buildings with on-site wetlands and botanical gardens recovering nutrients from circulating water. Fresh air, flowering plants and daylight everywhere. Beauty and comfort for every inhabitant. Rooftops covered in soil and sedum nourished by falling rain. Birds nesting and feeding in the building's verdant footprint. Imagine, in short, buildings as life-support systems in harmony with energy flows, human souls and other living things.

Inspired by the Hannover Principles, architects at WM+P have already designed buildings such as these. From an environmental studies center on the campus of Oberlin College to the corporate offices of Gap Inc.; from the Herman Miller "GreenHouse," a factory where you feel you've spent your day outdoors, to the Museum of Life and the Environment, which explores the deep connections between natural and cultural history both in the Appalachian Piedmont and beyond — designs by the architects at WM+P are testaments to the lively relationship between principles and practices.

And we are now seeing the Principles influence not just the work of WM+P, MBDC, and EPEA but a host of client companies. Ford Motor Company has launched the cradle-to-cradle renovation of its famous Rouge River industrial site with a new manufacturing facility, a factory with a living roof and a landscape of wetlands and swales that naturally purifies storm water runoff. Ford also introduced in 2003 the Model U, the world's first automobile designed to embrace the cradle-to-cradle vision.

Other business leaders are following suit. Shaw Industries, the largest producer of commercial carpet in the world, has begun to apply the Hannover Principles and cradle-to-cradle thinking to the company's product development process. Working with MBDC, Shaw is doing a scientific assessment of the material chemistry of its carpet fiber and backing to ensure that every ingredient is safe. The result: an infinitely recyclable, completely healthful carpet tile made from true technical nutrients that eliminate the concept of waste.

Working with the City of Chicago, WM+P drew upon the example of the Hannover Principles to serve Mayor Richard Daley's quest to make Chicago "the greenest city in America." The Chicago Principles, which will be announced in 2003, will provide a reference point as the City develops community plans and cradle-to-cradle systems that will make it a national model of how industry and ecology, nature and the city can flourish side by side.

There is really no end in sight — and that's the point. As we seek constant improvement by the sharing of knowledge, as our understanding of the world evolves, the Hannover Principles will continue to be our touchstone and inspiration for new designs. This process, merely a decade old, has already created hopeful changes in the world and is transforming the making of things into a regenerative force. Ultimately, we believe the principled practice of design will lead to ever more places and ever more products that honor not just human ingenuity but harmony with the exquisite intelligence of nature. And when *that* becomes the hallmark of good design, we will have entered a moment in human history when we can truly celebrate our kinship with all life.

FOUNDATIONS: DESIGN AND THE FORCES OF NATURE

The Hannover Principles are a set of maxims that encourage the design professions to take sustainability into consideration. They are descriptive of a way of thinking, not prescriptions or requirements. They take the form of a framework, based on the enduring elements of Earth, Air, Fire, Water, and Spirit, in which design decisions may be reviewed and evaluated. They are meant to guide our creative acts so that we may blend aesthetic concerns with ecological principles. In this way, design becomes a didactic tool, demonstrating that sustainable thinking can be put into practice in the real world.

The five elements provided a structure for the ancient world. The world can still be perceived along these lines, and they are presented here to frame the primary concerns of ecologically intelligent design.

Earth

In design, the earth is both the context and the material, the landscape and the things with which we build. Between context and material a balance must be struck that provides a meaningful and livable diversity of scale. A full range of experience from the "urban" to the "wild" is essential to the evolution of human culture.

Design solutions should benefit flora and fauna as much as humans, and the overall sense of connection between humanity and nature should be enhanced. A premium value should be placed on unbuilt space, particularly existing undeveloped lands. Reuse and expansion of the existing fabric may offer alternatives to new construction that will preserve the natural landscape.

New construction, when necessary, should be seen as an extension of the present built fabric, not as independent, self-contained development. Building materials need to be considered for their broadest range of effects—from emotive to practical—within a global and local context. Local production should be stressed, along with approaches that emphasize the regional, cultural and historical uniqueness of the place. Designers should consider the interaction and implementation of diverse materials within local climate and culture in a meaningful and productive way. They might consider the use of indigenous materials along with the practical and effective utilization of modern technology, including advanced glazing, energy-efficient fixtures and appliances, and nontoxic water treatment systems.

All materials can be considered in the following terms:

• Buildings should be designed to be flexible enough to accommodate many human purposes, including living, working or craft, allowing the materials to remain in place while serving different needs. Design should include alternatives for how the site can be adapted in the future.

- Materials should be considered in light of their sustainability: their process of extraction, manufacture, transformation and degradation through proper resource management on a global and local scale. All materials should be considered in terms of their embodied energy and characteristics of toxicity, potential off-gassing, finish and maintenance requirements.

- Products used should not be tested on animals.

- Recycling of materials is essential. But recycling should not be encouraged if materials come from products designed for disposability (compostable fabric, for example). If possible, provision should be made for manufacturers to disassemble and reuse all products. The reuse of entire structures must be considered in the event that buildings fail to be adaptable to future human needs.

- Materials should be chosen that minimize hazardous chemicals.

- Solid waste must be dealt with in a nontoxic manner. In nature, waste equals food. The aim is to eliminate any waste that cannot be shown to be part of a naturally sustainable cycle.

- Life cycle analysis of all materials and processes is important. Life cycle analysis is a process in which the energy use and environmental impact of the entire life cycle of the product, process, or activity is cataloged and analyzed. The life cycle encompasses extraction and processing of raw materials, manufacturing, transportation and maintenance, recycling and return to the environment.

- The design should qualify the environmental and economic costs so that the benefit of the project in relation to the expense is understood in both the short and long terms.

Air

Air is the element whose degradation we can sense most immediately. When the quality of the air is poor, all can feel it. Local atmospheric pollution may have global consequences, so the overall design must not contribute to further atmospheric denigration of any kind. Designs must be evaluated in terms of their atmospheric effects, including effects on ozone depletion and global warming. Alteration of the microclimate is equally significant. Any possibility for the design to counterbalance or contribute to remediation of existing environmental damage should be explored.

- Air-pollution implications of all design systems should be considered in the evaluation of designs. General air-quality issues should also be considered to insure that no off-site or on-site air pollution results from the design.

- Wind patterns in all seasons should be evaluated for both detrimental and beneficial effects on site configuration.

- Noise pollution should be accounted for and minimized.

- Building design must accommodate ventilation systems that meet specific air-quality needs. This may involve strategies that show concern for dangerous outdoor air conditions as well as efficient indoor air exchange.

- Natural ventilation patterns should be considered at every scale from the urban to the domestic as an alternative to artificial climate control.

- The health effects from indoor air-quality problems must be considered during the design process.

Fire

Fire is the most dramatic symbol of the human ability to harness natural energy. Energy is required to achieve comfort and convenience and to transform materials to useful effect. Designers are encouraged to invest their designs with the ability to operate based on on-site renewable energy sources, insofar as is possible, without reliance on fossil fuels or remote electrical generation. It is possible, given technologies and materials available today, to create buildings that maintain comfort levels passively without fossil fuels. This should be considered a minimum condition of energy design.

- Designs should interact with renewable natural energy flows. Solar energy should be evaluated in terms of its efficiency as well as the ways in which inhabitants and visitors enjoy the sunlight throughout the annual cycle. This implies an understanding of solar access and care for proper screening and shading techniques.

- Possibilities for on-site energy production must be considered, and accommodations should be incorporated into design.

- Buildings should, wherever possible, be net exporters of energy.

- Water heating shall be from renewable resources and be efficiently incorporated into the design.

- Transportation requirements should be considered in terms of their impact on overall energy consumption. Pedestrians and bicyclists should have priority. Mass transit should be efficient and available, and private automobile use should be discouraged. Allowances for automobiles should be carefully considered for their present and future implications with regard to energy use, urban planning and social effect. Auto services should anticipate alternative fuel strategies.

- The relationship between the design and the power grid should be considered. Minimum impact on energy demand from the grid is a goal; the value of decentralized energy sources should also be considered.

- The energy "embodied" in the building materials can have a significant impact on the energy consumption of the project. Embodied energy refers to all the energy necessary to extract, refine, transform and utilize the materials.

Water

Water is the most basic element of life on the planet and can be celebrated as a fundamental life-giving resource. Opportunities to create understanding, appreciation and enjoyment of water throughout the design of buildings, infrastructure and landscapes are encouraged. Designs should recognize the communal, cultural, historical, spiritual and poetic possibilities of the use of water and its central role as a precondition for life.

- Water use must be carefully accounted for throughout the entire design process.

- Water sources must be protected from contamination and careful consideration given to efficiency techniques at every step.

- Potable water should only be used for life-sustaining functions.

- Water from aquifers, rainwater, surface runoff water, gray water, and any water used for sewage transport or processing systems should all be considered within a cyclical concept.

- Wastewater must be returned to the earth in a beneficial manner. Organic treatment systems should be considered.

- No ground water contamination should result from any use of water resources related to the construction or operation of any of the project's facilities.

- Design shall consider rainwater and surface runoff water as possible resources for inhabitants and in building systems.

- Design should minimize impermeable ground cover.

- Gray water can be treated and applied to practical or natural purposes suitable to its characteristics.

- Water used in any process-related activity shall be put back into circulation, and toxic chemicals or heavy metals should be minimized. All discharges of process-related water shall meet drinking-water standards.

- Water, if used for sewage treatment or transportation, shall be restored to drinking-water standards prior to distribution or reuse.

Spirit

This most ineffable of elements is also the most human. Concern for sustainability is more than a matter of compliance with industrial regulation or environmental impact analysis. It embraces a commitment to conceive of design in the context of time, place and principled action, which implies accepting the value of all life and the rightful human place in nature. To understand kinship with all of life, people must be able to experience firsthand the feeling of belonging to the Earth in a particular place. Designing and living in sustainable architecture honors our place in the world; mediating human purpose and the needs of nature, it models a reciprocal relationship between people and their surroundings.

The presence of spirit ensures that design will be seen as only part of the solution to the world's problems. Spirit evokes humility, a sense of awe in the majesty of life. Adopting the principle of humility, designers can come to understand the inherent limitations of directing both human desires and natural processes. Design may encourage a sense of permanence and community, but it cannot legislate it. Similarly, our current understanding of the laws of nature cannot be the only criterion for evaluating a design. But design solutions can present an aesthetic statement that engages society in honoring and more deeply understanding the human place in the natural world.

THE MEANING OF SUSTAINABILITY

HISTORICAL, ECOLOGICAL AND PHILOSOPHICAL ROOTS

William McDonough + Partners with David Rothenberg

Sustainability is a loaded and slippery term. It names those activities that can be continued far into the future, defining a way of life that will last. The trouble is, it's nothing new. Business and industry have always hoped that whatever course they choose will be the sustainable course, one that will not push them out of business. From this perspective, sustainability can add up to very little that actually supports human society and the natural world.

But there is no practical advantage gained by scolding business too much. Indeed, if environmental and social woes are to be effectively addressed, our solutions will have to encourage business activity rather than forbid it. Even so, business will not change overnight. Will it change fast enough to respond to ecological needs? We don't know. But understanding what we mean by sustainability, understanding the roots of our desire for change, may help us craft design solutions that generate real movement toward a prosperous and truly sustainable future.

Sustainable Development?

"Sustainable development" implies a kind of growth that will be able to go on and on. But some would suggest the terms are mutually exclusive. How much development, ultimately, is truly sustainable? Will there come a time when we will have to chastise growth itself? The industrial community certainly hopes that will never be so. And that is why the Brundtland Commission couches the definition of sustainable development so carefully.

According to the Commission, sustainable development means "meeting the needs of the present while not compromising the ability of the future to meet its own needs." If humans in the future decide it is time to forsake the earth, this definition says nothing to stop it. The phrase is intentionally weak, to garner wide acceptance. It says: Don't force our children to regret the past; at least make it possible for future societies to have a choice.

A reasonable step, as far as it goes. But, as World Bank economist Herman Daly points out, some definitions of sustainability are patently counterproductive. They include "sustainable development is development that sustains the highest rate of economic growth without inflation." That's just business as usual, described a little differently, so that our present notion of growth stays on course. Another is: "Sustainability considers the expanding needs of a growing world population, implying a steady and necessary growth." This suggests that development will need to be continuous and expanding, regardless of the earth's limits. Finding formulations like these woefully inadequate, Daly proposes three specific rules to make sense of sustainability in economic terms:

1. Harvest renewable resources only at the speed at which they regenerate.

2. Limit wastes to the assimilative capacity of local ecosystems.

3. Require that part of the profit be put aside for investment in a renewable substitute resource.

Furthermore, sustainable development does not follow from more free trade across global lines. For a nation to create a sustainable economy, Daly writes, it must step back from the global economy. Sustainability begins on a smaller scale, emerging in local experiments, not in law. This is the remarkable potential of EXPO 2000. Imagined as a community experiment, it can be a model of what a sustainable settlement might look like in our increasingly complicated world.

Traditional Settlements, Planetary Culture

Examples of sustainability are not hard to cull from the history of world cultures. Most often they are small-scale social solutions that involve a limited number of people who do little or no damage to their surrounding habitat. Typically, there is no design or designer that guides the inhabitation of the place. But this is rarely true anymore. The interactions between people and nature have grown so complex, the rate and scale of change so overwhelming, we can no longer rely on setting up benign situations and letting innovative solutions slowly evolve. Design has become crucial to our future — and to achieve any measure of sustainability we are in need of designs that strike a balance between the local and the global, traditional settlements and the emerging planetary culture.

We find hopeful, if distant, examples of sustainable design in works such as Bernard Rudofsky's *Architecture without Architects*, which presents villages, cities, fortresses, and monasteries from traditional cultures across the globe. In these traditional settlements, buildings are arranged so that the flows of wind are channeled and harnessed, not blocked and diverted. It is clear that these places have been blessed with the luxury of time; no one commissioned these structures and demanded that they be quickly built and ready for use. Intervention was slow enough to be tested by the strength of natural forces and the sobering spirit of time. The result: long-enduring structures that suggest that sustainable building relies less on an absolute coherent plan than on the cooperation between designers, inhabitants and the forces of nature.

In traditional cultures, designers and inhabitants were often the same people. In the Himalayas, for example, the mostly stone houses are never considered fixed, finished buildings. They evolve as the inhabitants change, with new rooms and structures built out from existing walls, gradually forming an irregular urban fabric in which no angle is exactly ninety degrees and no street follows an exact grid, even though these principles may have had a hand in the original thought behind the town. Similarly, the beloved and varied landscape of European country villages was not planned by any overseeing authority but developed slowly and tentatively. Communities organized themselves, and each environmental intervention took much longer than it does today. Change was not rapid, but it was always part of the plan.

When we ask for a design cognizant of long-term sustainability, we want buildings that will be able to adapt; we mean designs that do not legislate so much that what is not known today will be made invisible in the future. The plan must leave room for the changing understanding of humanity's place in the natural world.

This does not mean designers should eschew innovation and technology for a traditionalist stance. The forthcoming Agenda 21 document, which will be the main policy statement from the June UNCED conference in Brazil, suggests why this is so. It states:

> By the year 2025, 60% of the Earth's population will live in cities. Degradation of the environment and human living conditions is already seen in cities, particularly in developing countries. Cities also generate 60% of gross national

product worldwide, and can develop the capacity to sustain their productivity.

Proposals the United Nations is considering focus on sustainable planning and management methods that will meet the housing, water, sanitation, safety, and waste management needs for billions of people.

Solutions to problems caused by human settlements are linked to issues of energy, air, and water on a global scale. International organizations and funding sources should provide both human and financial resources. Traditionally, funding for human settlements has been low.

(Section I, Chapter 6 of Agenda 21; document A/CONF.151 /PC/100/Add.7).

Though somewhat vague, the statement illustrates why the sustainable settlements of the future will need to be very different from the beautiful, organic examples of vernacular architecture from around the world. The human impact on the environment is global in scope. The greenhouse effect and the widening ozone hole are two graphic and unintended consequences of worldwide industrialization. No one planned them, yet they are the clear result of our global energy interventions.

So, a way of life based on buildings that will last and evolve must also consider the full range of local events that contribute to global environmental conditions. The planetary must be combined with the regional. This is a standard by which picturesque examples of traditional communities cannot be judged, but it is one to which new developments should aspire. Each new development we begin today is going to be enmeshed in a global network of resource use as well as local energy flows — a dual condition that was never true of any Italian hill town or Yemenite fortress. From this perspective, it becomes clear why eliminating the concept of waste and relying on the energy of the sun are crucial principles for building sustainable settlements in a planetary culture.

Ecology and Sustainability

Caring for the Earth, the strategy for sustainability published by the International Union for the Conservation of Nature (IUCN), takes an ecological tack in defining sustainable development. According to IUCN, sustainability implies "improving the quality of human life while living within the carrying capacity of supporting ecosystems." Carrying capacity is not static. A less industrial culture with high population growth and density will make different demands on an ecosystem than an industrialized culture with a more stable population and a much higher per capita energy use. *World Resources 1992–93* notes some of the ways in which resource use and carrying capacity need to be explored:

> Sustainable development necessitates protecting the natural resources needed for food production and cooking fuels, while expanding produc-

tion to meet the needs of growing populations. These are potentially conflicting goals, and yet failure to conserve the natural resources on which agriculture depends would ensure future shortages of food. Sustainable development means more efficient use of arable lands and water supplies, as well as development and adoption of improved agricultural practices and technologies to increase yields. It aims to avoid overuse of chemical fertilizers and pesticides, so that they do not degrade rivers and lakes, threaten wildlife, and contaminate human food and water supplies. It means careful use of irrigation, to avoid waterlogging of cropland. It means avoiding the expansion of agriculture into marginal soils that would rapidly erode.

Clearly, the full environmental impact of each human intervention must be considered at every step of development if we are to build societies that thrive within the limits of the natural world. This is especially true for designers and planners involved with the Hannover Expo, who will have to carefully consider the impact of millions of visitors on a fragile, heavily populated region.

Indeed, considering Germany as a whole suggests the importance of an ecological perspective. With a population of 77,573,000, Germany is the twelfth largest country in the world. At 1.4 trillion dollars, it is fourth highest in GNP, and at 1.14 billion tons CO_2 equivalent, the country is sixth highest in greenhouse gas emissions. With a land area of only 137, 801 square miles, Germany is the fifty-seventh largest country on the planet. The incongruity of population and available land makes environmental pressures among the country's top concerns. Most of Germany is part of the temperate forest biome, which covers only 4 percent of the world's surface, despite its preference by humans as habitat. So from the point of view of other species in this type of community, preserving forests is of utmost importance. Forest damage from acid rain is visible throughout the nation, and as much as 50 percent of all trees are thought to be damaged. Heavy metals and toxic effluents lace the waters, and air quality is often threatened. And much of the wooded area is so rigorously managed that nothing near the optimal level of biodiversity is encouraged.

An example of the possible ecological richness this habitat could sustain may be found in Poland's Bialowieza National Park, an area of 47.4 square kilometers protected by a buffer zone of managed forest 15 kilometers wide. Among the mammals thriving there are lynx, wolf, wild boar, elk, red deer, roe deer, and the celebrated European bison, reintroduced after near extinction in 1929. The unique value of this fragment of an ancient forest has been appreciated by the nation under successive forms of government, and is respected around the world as well.

From the Urban to the Wild

A well-rounded culture offers a full range of landscape experience, from the urbane to the wild. As people interact with a diversity of landscapes over time, the human ecology of a place begins to emerge. Unfortunately, attempts to plan for diversity and encourage contact with the natural world have usually legislated too much, imposing rather than suggesting a particular relationship with locale. It all ends up looking far too artificial.

Perhaps the most famous planning effort of this kind in modern times is the garden cities movement. Led by Ebenezer Howard, the garden cities movement tried to specify not only the physical layout of the ideal urban form, it also took a stab at defining the socioeconomic and philosophical basis for a modern way of life that would bring its inhabitants into contact with nature even as industrialization grew. Agriculture and industry were to be linked in a design where financial equity would be shared with residents. The socialists Charles Fourier and Robert Owen had come up with similar ideas in the middle of the nineteenth century, but they usually envisioned a single building surrounded by productive land. Not having firsthand experience with building the environment, their ideas were more sophisticated than their models. Howard's visions were diagrammatic and geometric, not so much specifying building type as how open space, streets, and built sections were to be laid out. The idea was socialist, but the picture was orderly and somewhat totalitarian. The notion that new developments could be conceived not as suburban sprawl, but as independent, self-sufficient communities offered a profound alternative to the rapidly growing urban centers. Here is how Howard described Welwyn, a garden city seen as a satellite of London, in 1919:

> The town will be laid out on garden city principles, the town area being defined and the rest of the estate permanently preserved as an agricultural and rural belt. Particular care will be taken, in the arrangement of the town, to reduce internal transport and transit, whether of factory and office workers, or of goods, to the practicable minimum. A population of 40-50,000 will be provided for, efforts being made to anticipate all its social, recreative, and civic needs. The aim is to create a self-contained town, with a vigorous life of its own independent of London.

Though garden cities did try to mix housing, workplaces, and commerce, it was wrong to imagine that they could be closed systems, autonomous and detached from the rest of suburban sprawl. Macroeconomic catastrophes like the Great Depression began to undermine their fiscal health, and it was difficult to maintain co-ownership over any length of time. Welwyn was eventually taken over by a developer, and now it is primarily a residential suburb. Another of Howard's garden cities at the outskirts of Oslo,

Norway, at Ulleval, originally conceived as worker housing, is now considered so picturesque that only the most wealthy can afford to live there. That is a mark of both its success and its failure: Superior to the more lifeless suburbs that followed it, the garden cities now are valued nostalgically, more as places of residential luxury than anything else. They had the forces of a growing economic system against them, and they had to defer to external demographic change before their own sustainability could be tested.

The great modernist Le Corbusier had his own principles for how the city could embrace its location, and they do not seem so different from the kind of things proposed today:

1. We must decongest the center of our cities.
2. We must augment their density.
3. We must increase the means for getting about.
4. We must increase parks and open spaces.

So much for principles! The problem lies in the lack of concern for the "edges" between these conflicting aims, and the street separation between the parts of the plan. Le Corbusier enjoyed huge high-rises overlooking open countryside, and when you look at the places where he was allowed free reign, such as the new cities he designed in northern India, you see the imposed, exact geometry of modernism turning away from a nature left unconsidered outside the city walls. This kind of rigid separation encourages the idea that human interests are separate from natural interests and will always conflict. Such a division precludes a creative solution, and speaks again for the virtue of modesty in urban planning. Lewis Mumford later called Le Corbusier's well-articulated vision the picture of the "anti-city":

> The first mistake was the overvaluation of mechanization and standardization as ends in themselves without respect for human purpose. The second was the theoretical destruction of every vestige of the past, without preserving any links in form or visible structure between past and future, thereby magnifying the importance of the present and at the same time threatening with destruction whatever permanent values the present might in turn create....This is the error of the disposable urban container. Finally Corbusier's concept carried to its extreme the necessary reaction against urban overcrowding: the mistake of separating and extravagantly over-spacing facilities whose topographic proximity is essential for their daily use.

Le Corbusier's greatest contribution to planning was to liberate the plan from preconditioned constraints. With the new materials of reinforced concrete and steel, he demonstrated that whole new environments could be conceived, based on the designer's experience of the site. His best work is on a smaller scale, where the sculptural nature of his architecture defines fascinating spaces. He just tried to expand these ideas too far, beyond the limits of their indifference to context. And yet the mainstream application of his ideas proved even worse than the monumental models: Suburbia, as it has turned out lacks any organic focus because it is seen as a place to live, not to work, thereby separating livelihood from home. How could anything but alienation result?

The backlash to the sterility of New Town theory can be said to have begun with the work of Jane Jacobs, who argues as a writer from outside the architectural profession that the congestion and mixed use of older cities supports a vitality and genuine community that planned cities do not. The original city was based on the intermingling of people from different social classes and the cultural value of chance meetings in streets with a past. Can such a traditional way of life be simulated? A successful community needs a *locus mundi* where an identifiable center for human interaction and interchange is scaled to social and cultural demographics. There needs to be a "well point" where unplanned communication can occur.

Is the recovery of tradition compatible with the ecological imperatives of using solar-based renewable energy and eliminating the concept of waste? The planners who build on Jacobs's approach, such as Leon Krier, Peter Calthorpe, and Andres Duany and Elizabeth Plater-Zyberk, are less motivated by ecological worry than by the social boredom of most post –World War II building worldwide. There are so many aspects involved in design that even well-intentioned planning strategies may go awry. It is important that design not constrain the human or natural economy; people should be free to determine spatial utility.

Design should never dictate. It should be didactic only as part of a larger environmental education. If ecological constraints are too strong, it may be best not to build anything new. Instead, designers might retrofit existing plans or structures, doing as little damage as possible while ensuring that the city allows for the presence of nature throughout its fabric. Corridors of green such as Frederick Law Olmstead's nineteenth-century "emerald necklace" in Boston now may be seen to have value for wildlife, not just for human enjoyment, but the strategy is still the same. A diversity of scales and habitats should be accessible to everyone and readily experienced in daily life.

It is a great challenge to link environmental conscience with enduring design. John Todd, founder of the New Alchemy Institute on Cape Cod, Massachusetts, has worked for several decades on "living machines" conceived as miniature earths containing many components of a food chain. More than greenhouses, they represent a synthesis of solar and wind energy, biology and electronics in a living ecosystem that cultivates food, purifies water and sustains a comfortable environment. Todd imagines them as an integral part of the future human world:

A living machine is a device made up of living organisms of all types, usually housed within a casing or structure of 'gossamer' materials. Like a conventional machine it is comprised of inter-related parts with separate functions and used in the performance of some type of work. …They are engineered with the same design principles used by nature to build and regulate its great ecologies in forests, lakes, prairies, or estuaries. Their primary energy source is sunlight. Like the planet they have hydrological and mineral cycles. They are, however, totally new, contained environments.

The full expression of the living machines is far from being realized. I predict that it will become an integral part of the architecture and design of towns, villages, and city neighborhoods. Urban agriculture will be widespread and productive. Sewage will be treated and recycled in living machines. With plants, animals, soil, water, and purifying gases, these structures will become the workhorses of a solar age.

The following table demonstrates how living machines differ from conventional technologies with regard to energy use:

	Living Machines	**Conventional Technology**
Primary Energy Sources	the sun	fossil fuel, nuclear power
Secondary Sources	radiant energy internal biogenesis of gases	combustion and electricity
Capture of External Energy	intrinsic to design	rare
Internal Storage	heat, nutrients, and gases	batteries
Efficiency	low biological transfer efficiency in subsystems, high in overall aggregate efficiency	high in best technologies, low when total infrastructure is calculated
Lifespan	long, to centuries	short, to decades
Recycling	internal and intrinsic	pollution control devices if anything
Material	parts are living populations	hardware-based

These comparisons suggest the goals of such technology, but it requires creative understanding on the part of the designer to create real places from such organic devices. Visiting Bali with anthropologist Margaret Mead, Todd experienced villages that fused practical, artistic, and religious elements in their everyday relations with the natural world. He realized that the organic constructions he was trying to envision as part of a city were too individually conceived; they were more like single buildings than whole plans addressing the complex ways people live. The ecological imperative fails if used to replace architecture rather than supplement it. The designer's challenge is to combine engineering philosophy with aesthetic and stylistic planning constraints.

Appropriate solutions also involve a certain specific attention to the site at hand. Local knowledge is essential to guarantee ecologically aware designs. Roberto Burle Marx, celebrated Brazilian landscape architect, uses 50,000 species of plants rather than the 12,000 species of the European world. This respect for the great tropical diversity leads to an ecological sensibility:

> People are so uneducated. Nature is always destroyed in the name of progress. Nature is a cycle of life that you must understand in order to take liberties with it in good conscience. The means at our disposal like the great bulldozers, fire, defoliants, can just as well be used for good

as for evil but in Brazil they are used to create misery.

But this ecology is not extremist: "I don't say that in my gardens I don't plant foreign plants — I do. *But they must fit into our landscape.* It is important that a design is a result of our existing landscape and flora."

In most cases, the traditional division between settlement, agricultural, and forestry land-use patterns may be preserved. If care is taken with the existing landscape, its features may be preserved as new development is put on the site. However, in Germany it may be useful to take an over managed monoculture forest and change it into a mixed stand simply to demonstrate the failings of previously restrictive forest management.

A truly sustainable community will need to be far more integrated than most planning or environmental experiments to date. An inspiring example is Curitiba, Brazil, a city of 1.6 million inhabitants that has made environmental concerns a priority of development. High-rise development is encouraged only in structural axes with central, special lanes for buses. Instead of huge, expensive downtown renewal projects, the city has favored small-scale projects that preserve traditional localities and as much parkland as possible. Individual families are encouraged to separate trash for recycling by garbage-for-food programs in the poorer parts of town. Environmental education is instituted at all school levels. As a result of its commitment to providing a high quality of life, the city is a favored site for new industries of local and foreign origin.

It is not design's place to create a religion of appropriate habitation, but that may be happening of its own accord as attention to ecology becomes a fact of our present life, much like attention to progress was earlier in this century. Ecological thinking must not become too thin and scattered. It is an important aspect of life, but not a self-contained "new system." Design can teach a practical involvement with natural cycles as well as an aesthetic celebration of the range of possible ways to live outward into the natural and social world. It need never hide the individual in a sealed box of his own making.

The Evolution of the Industrial Age

Most thinking on the relationship between humanity and nature tends to separate us from our surroundings. The constraints in our language are often to blame; the words we have are "humanity" and "nature." But the problem of sustainability can be solved only by redefining humanity within the realm of the natural world, by understanding where we are and how we can enhance and preserve our sense of place. To come to terms with the problem, we might investigate how separating people and nature has led to the disastrous developments of recent history.

Ecological degradation is nothing unique to modern times. Plato lamented the total deforestation of the

Greek isles. Whole Middle Eastern civilizations were brought to ruin after water supplies ran out. The cliff dwellings of Mesa Verde in Colorado were abandoned after a twenty-year drought. With the onset of the industrial revolution, humanity began to move farther away from a sustainable path as technology accelerated change and societies adopted principles that worked for industry but disrupted human life and the cycles of the natural world. From this crucible emerged the ideas that would coalesce into our contemporary understanding of sustainability.

Despite misuse by political forces, the social analysis of Karl Marx remains a profound attempt to address the split between people and nature. Marx, for example, explained how the typical factory worker, making fragments of larger objects that he would never have any use for, was alienated from the fruits of his labors. The forces of industry, meanwhile, separated many facets of everyday life, removing action from an embracing context. Marx called for "production in a human manner," work in which we share and give of ourselves through the things we design and build. No plan would be imposed on another, and each creation would fulfill itself by connecting each maker to another and to the world as a whole. The failure of these ideas in the hardscrabble world is testament to the path the modern era chose to follow.

Martin Heidegger placed the roots of our detachment in the moment we began to extract energy from nature, storing it to be consumed at will with no sense of the earth's cycles. When energy is seen as a "standing-reserve," the concept of waste is inherent, because energy is regarded as something to be used up. The world is no longer something to partake in; it is a supply for consumption. This approach has fueled industrial progress, but has not fostered a way of life that sustains society within the limits of nature.

Lewis Mumford made famous the goal of a post-industrial, progressive culture that would respect the value of organic cycles. His categorization of history is pertinent to designers. He puts forth a conception of three great phases in technology: the eotechnic, the paleotechnic, and the neotechnic. The first extends roughly to 1750, the second runs through the industrial revolution until the turn of our century, and the third gathers momentum in the 1920s and 1930s, extrapolating promise into generations to follow.

The eotechnic is marked by handicraft and agriculture, labors that embody human participation in the environment. By expanding human presence outward, this phase enhanced human life by harnessing the immanent natural forces that surround us. Water, wood, and stone are the dominant materials. Tools are manufactured by craftspeople for specific tasks and easily customized by the user. Mumford saw this phase as generally positive, a time when technology enriched the life of the senses through direct perceptual extensions like the telescope. It was also characterized by developments in urban and garden design, and the artistic depiction of daily existence. We expressed ourselves in nature's terms and did not focus on the control of our habitat for our own ends.

Why did we move on? According to Mumford, the change began in England, somewhat at the fringes of the eotechnic world, when population increased dramatically in the nineteenth century and the old agricultural order could not be sustained. At about the same time, it became economically feasible to consume energy generated by coal. The new industries that arose were not based on enhancing life but on carbon-fueled inventions like the steam engine and the railroad. Suddenly, human presence was expanded into nature through powerful machines, and life became ever more quantified and driven. In effect, workers suffered to make industry grow, and the physical environment was sacrificed as well. According to Mumford's compelling but somewhat romantic view, it was capital that drove this march into squalor.

For Mumford, this period was not the culmination of human innovation; it was a preliminary phase in which human strength is tested against nature. That's why he calls the industrial age the paleotechnic era, a passing phase in which quality of life was sacrificed to further technology. To transcend the paleotechnic, Mumford suggested that we should step back from its unique brutality to affirm organic human values in a living world.

Pre–World War II optimism renewed faith in technology as a natural force. Human culture would find a way to progress and at the same time support life. Mumford called the prewar years the neotechnic era, a time when technology would fulfill its original purpose by bringing humanity and the world back together. This was the era of electricity, social engineering, efficiency, and the birth of instantaneous communication; the period when the machine begins to arc back and affect human essence in more profound ways. Cooperative thought, the functionalist aesthetic, and a more balanced, material sense of human personality are some of the effects of mechanization upon the mind. Comprehension of the modern machine makes order accessible to all, no longer the sole privilege of an industrial complex ruled from above.

Mumford is not naive enough to claim our progression toward the renewal of humanity with the aid of the machine to be an absolute democratic goal. Even in his steadfast belief that the machine may be inducted into the service of life, nature is never to be wholly independent of human inquiry:

> We may arbitrarily define nature as that part of our experience which is neutral to our desires and interests: but we…have been formed by nature and inescapably are part of the system of nature. Once we have picked and chosen from this realm, as we do in science, the result is a

work of art — our art: certainly it is no longer in a state of nature.

Mumford implores us to assimilate the mechanical virtues of impersonality, objectivity, and neutrality before we sail toward the edge of a more richly organic, more profoundly human civilization that returns to the virtues of life. What evidence does he give us to support the conclusion that technology has changed enough to suggest goals beyond itself? Machinery itself, Mumford writes, is no longer composed of standardized, identical units that are pieced together. Instead, individual parts are specialized, refined, made more particularly precise to fit into the whole and achieve meaning in the great technical system.

Earlier machinery needed to simplify organic processes to render them in mechanical form. Neotechnic mechanical parts become more complicated individually, mirroring the complexity of the species and niches of the natural world. The game of machines is no longer like checkers, with teams of identical pieces; it is like chess, complex and regulated. The goal: dissolving the rigid mechanical world picture and redirecting humanity toward an organic understanding, quantifiable only in terms of growth and change. The shift toward the natural in technology begins when we see machinery not as the towering achievement of an ingenious humanity, but as "lame counterfeits of living organisms." What is an airplane next to an eagle, a radio next to the voice?

Our proudest technical achievements only approximate the organic functionalism within nature. By reconsidering the wonder of natural processes, human techniques can be rejuvenated.

Mumford's utopia has yet to emerge — which could be seen as cause for relief. With hindsight, Mumford's technical vision and his illustrations of an "organic" architecture "harmonizing" humanity and nature, begin to appear suspect. A photograph of boxlike, concrete, single-room dwellings for Swedish workers framed against an evergreen forest is touted as a "handsome and well-integrated human environment, in which the efficiency of neotechnical production can be registered in a higher standard of living and a wider use of leisure." From today's perspective, it looks like a row of mobile homes parked at the edge of the wilderness, ruining the view and reducing biodiversity. A hydropower station seems as rectilinear and devoid of affinity with nature as any concrete skyscraper glimpsed across a prairie. The scale of the place alone is enough to suggest certain environmental disaster. Yet for Mumford it is a "symbol of a fresh mode of thinking and feeling." To our eyes it looks like a piece of empty, colorless industrial architecture, built with little attention to its place.

Mumford reevaluated technology at the end of his life. Despite all his encouraging 1930s rhetoric, our built environment had failed to become conversant with nature. Design may have looked organic, but it rarely avoided harming the natural world. Early twentieth century attempts to build in harmony with nature—including Mumford's own—were too dependent on the metaphors of engineering. The idea of efficiency, of minimizing this or maximizing that, reinforces the limitations of mechanistic thinking, which imagines everything we do or experience to be part of a quantifiable system. Perhaps we can begin to invite into our designs those forbidden aspects of nature and experience: the unplanned, the fortuitous, the places evolving free of imposed ideas. The best solution may not always be the shortest route from point A to point B.

When we recognize the failures of modernism and industrialization, various possible paths emerge. There is the optimistic idea of an ultra-high-tech industry, based not on resource exploitation but on electronic notions of work and creation. In the ineffable realm of cyberspace, humanity would metamorphose and no longer depend on the physical. There is also the Arcadian dream of a return to an earlier time, a simpler and more "natural" way of life.

None of these visions, however hopeful and well-intentioned, confronts the realities of our time. To do so, design thinking needs to add up to more than eco- or techno-rhetoric. The idea of making human creation part of nature is as old as Aristotle, but the meaning of the goal has changed as we have become more aware of the fragility and interdependence of natural systems. As our knowledge grows, we must continue to refine our understanding of sustainability so that our designs can contribute to a life-affirming relationship between people and the natural world.

Rights and Responsibilities: The Ecological Ethics of Intelligent Design

The history of the concept of "right" shows an expansion of those considered to be worthy of equal moral consideration. It was once common to accept slavery in many societies, and only recently have equal rights been extended to women in political and social matters. Now we speak of extending the concept of rights far enough to include animals, plants, and ecosystems, which have a right to their own fulfillment, independent of what we may use them for.

This does not mean staying out of nature's way as much as possible — increasing world population and the very notion of development preclude this — but rather, accepting the inherent, intrinsic value of nature. Immanuel Kant thought we should "never use a person only as a means." Contemporary ecophilosopher Arne Naess expands this to state: "Never use a living being only as a means." We cannot avoid incorporating people or living beings into our schemes, but we are capable of respecting their value beyond our immediate requirements.

The consequences of this expansion of right into nature are very simple: *Design for the needs of all species.* If some facets of a design are of no value to people but support the rest of nature, that is well and good. A swamp that supports an astounding diversity of life may be more valuable than the pretty, managed marsh. And if we choose to sequester some areas as undisturbed natural habitat, recognize that the setting up of boundaries is itself a human disturbance whose effects need to be understood.

The use of ecological sustainability as a guiding direction for design can be taken in two different ways, following the two kinds of environmental philosophy known as deep ecology and social ecology. Deep ecology tends to believe the denuding of the earth will be prevented by a change in mindset and in values, while social ecology asserts that the structures of society need to be totally revamped before we can even imagine what improvement might look like. The former is favored by philosophers, eco-activists, and environmental consultants who believe that changing individual minds is the key to changing the world. The latter appeals to social planners and activists of the class struggle who see people primarily as products of the social systems they are born into. The choice is between articulating a strong idea of what values environmentalism should hold on to and looking for a reconception of social systems that might prevent ecological devastation from continuing at its present rate.

Deep ecology is well articulated by philosopher Paul Taylor, whose central goal is to establish respect for nature as a guiding ethical standard built on the principle of respect for human life. Arne Naess, who coined the term "deep ecology" and has been named its philosophical grandfather, thinks intuition about the intrinsic value of all nature will ground a respectful way of living in and with the natural, non-human world. Taylor demands a rational structure to articulate the bounds of respect for the world outside our own species' goals and dreams. To bridge these views, he asks: "What is the ethical significance of our being members of the Earth's community of life?"

The natural science of ecology may serve to bring into focus the relationships between human beings and other components of the biosphere, but it will never tell us what to do about these relationships. As a natural science, it has difficulty dealing with a full spectrum of human values. To decide how to act is up to us as people, as moral agents. This is where philosophy is meant to help us: It can offer suggestions for how to act in the context of a new ecological perspective, giving scientists a framework for taking moral considerations into account — even if those considerations are outside the assumed bounds of their profession.

Respect for nature is not the same as love of nature. It is not just affection or care. Respect, says Taylor, is a public and moral commitment. It demands the definition of rules and standards. In loving nature you embrace all the uncertainty and tumult of the wild while admitting its necessity for your survival. But respect is a question of treating the other fairly, and this is where specific ethical considerations are critical. These might include real, tangible ways to evaluate competing claims of environmental responsibility.

Taylor analyzed competing interests by measuring the ways in which conflicting parties expressed principles of self-defense, proportionality, minimum wrong, and distributive justice. With emphasis on human/nonhuman conflicts, he finds that dissent may be the norm in human contact with the rest of the world. We have to think sometimes for ourselves, and sometimes for the rest of nature. Even when acting with a spirit of respect, we cannot do right by all things all the time.

Deep ecologists tend to take insights from the natural science of ecology and then wonder what changes in human forms of thought will be necessary to appreciate them. Yet this may be too short a step. Perhaps the metaphors from ecology offer more pertinent challenges to the whole manner in which we conceive our communal existence. Rather than assume that nature is good and reorient our beliefs to reflect this, we might take the definitions of life and interconnectedness offered by scientific ecology as preliminary hints for a new way of seeing society. This represents not a new vision of a better society, but a new device for understanding what we have.

This is the view of Niklas Luhmann in his *Ecological Communication*. A social theorist in the German critical tradition, Luhmann is quick to caution against laying too much weight on any shared moral consensus in our time. There are just too many different kinds of people with different wants and needs; real agreement on the highest goals and value systems is not very likely. A principle like "respect for nature" will never mean only one thing to all people. Instead, ecology can offer new methods to take stock of the differences in human activities and situations. It can offer new conceptions of existing society, necessary before any realistic goal may be articulated.

Environmental ethics, according to Luhmann, is most often a rhetoric of anxiety. It gets us worked up and nervous about the end of the earth, just as we make moral pronouncements that the current course of human progress is wrong. But to what extent are environmental problems moral problems at all? It is not a question of individuals believing the wrong things, but of social systems doing real damage to the world in which we live.

Environmental ethics tends to shy away from the revelation of what's wrong with the systems of civilization, taking refuge in uncertain hopes and fears. If you speak only of persons and not of society, you can only hope to change persons. And society is not a person that needs instruction or admonishment.

Luhmann's view is that we need to reconceive present society upon devices borrowed from ecology before we can know what a socially respectful eco-ethics could be. Why bring in these devices at all? Ecology has excelled at showing the relationships between previously unconnected aspects of the biosphere, and disparate parts of society might be linked in an analogous way. Ethicists too often assume the autonomy of the human and the natural, though society interactively defines the two. Consider the working of social systems upon emerging principles of natural systems, and the relationship may come clear.

Luhmann is intrigued by the concept of autopoiesis, or self-direction and renewal, a biological principle developed by Humberto Maturana and Francisco Varela. Maturana and Varela believe that autopoiesis is a criterion for life. The mechanical systems of cybernetics, invented by the early computer pioneers to suggest how machines might become self-regulating, could not renew or create themselves. Thus cybernetic automata could never quite achieve a "living" condition. In outlining the qualities of systems that refer to as well as regenerate themselves, these two contemporary biologists are attempting to model the elusive sense of what it means to be alive. Applying autopoiesis to social systems, Luhmann's vision is the latest instance of a long tradition of borrowing concepts from natural science for use in social rhetoric. He is often more careful than his predecessors, like Herbert Spencer, who drew quick moral conclusions from Darwinism rather than thoroughly rounding out a theory. For Luhmann, social systems remain "alive" if they continue to communicate, and the links between them make up a vast ecological network of relationships. There is an ecology of social structures as much as there is order in an ecosystem.

No part makes sense separate from its communications with the whole.

Autopoiesis is a code of social existence. Its operative meaning is to continue to communicate. When communication fails, the system becomes diseased, falling apart at its wounds. If the course of information goes smoothly, the defined "life" of social systems functions as an immune system to keep the ecology of society afloat. For example, polluting a water supply happens when we do not understand the adverse effects of an industry. If we find that the water is rendered unhealthy, we redesign the system so pollution is reduced.

Luhmann's concept of ecological communication is a theoretical schema intended to reveal how social systems respond to their contexts and why we usually fail to see the natural limitations of these organizations. Luhmann develops a very specific and somewhat mechanistic language to explain the way it all fits together. In a style typical of sociology, he models social reality as a series of codes and programs, connected to each other like some vague machinery whose invisible cogs reflect nature only as they simplify it. But he does place a limit on these social mechanics: We can never glimpse the whole from within the whole — inside the whale, Jonah does not know where he is.

Humility

With Jonah's predicament in mind, we might begin to consider the place of humility in architecture and design. Architects often make magnanimous pronouncements of how important their creations are to a new social vision, but rarely do they step back to realize that the built environment does not change everything. In fact, most of the world's best architecture is not designed by any single designer or planner; instead it represents a community solution to a variety of problems that are often better understood by diverse parts of the social fabric.

When we suggest humility, we mean leaving space for the design to evolve on its own. Leave room for the many important aspects of life not dictated by design. Leave room for a nature far greater than any notion of "closed-system," "feedback loop," "balanced ecology," "sublime wilderness," or any kind of ideal we may ascribe to it. José Ortega y Gasset wrote that modern man, what he called the "Mass Man," is unable to distinguish between a natural object and an artifact, because we do not need to question technology as we use it. When we get in the train, we assume it will take us to our destination. When we type at the computer, we assume words will appear on the screen. There is no need to know more about the tools that we use, and most of us do not understand them well enough to keep them in good repair.

These are the products of our design, and we cannot think about them too much if we are to use them successfully. We accept them, and we go on. It is the same with our artificial ideas of nature. We come up with truisms like balance and interdependence of nature, and then we step back from them, assuming we can exclude ourselves from the equation. Then we imagine nature as somehow contained in our simplistic analyses.

That misses the point. Nature is more than we can ever describe or know. Only a design that encourages future discovery will be able to ensure that we remember this. A design that plans too much will limit its expression to the current purview, shutting itself off to new insights about humanity's place in nature. Understanding is always on the move.

It is very difficult to introduce humility into prescriptions about the future, or into any plans that authorize a specific intervention into what exists in the environment. Scientific ecologists are used to saying things like "we simply do not know enough to be sure what course of action is best for the biosphere," but political and philosophical ecologists are quick to say "Design with nature! Follow the rules of balance and harmony so essential to the natural world!" One must be careful to mold these imperatives into methods truly usable, not just new dogmas to replace the old.

The evidence is clear from the record of our century: efforts to plan all aspects of the environment have failed. Neither previous world's fairs nor suburban sprawls were founded on evil intentions. It's just that their promoters were too sure of their ideology to be able to include a critique of their own ideas in the design process.

We need to find ways to recognize the absolute nature of the sustainable goal without turning our work into ideology. Here, architectural theorist Christopher Alexander's *Timeless Way of Building* may be of help. Rather than addressing the concepts of "nature" or "harmony" or "sense of community" he writes poetically of the "quality without a name," the essence of a place that can always be recognized by those who visit a landscape graced with ineffable beauty. Alexander circles around his subjects, Zen-like, rather than holding them up for critical examination: "It is a process which brings order out of nothing but ourselves; it cannot be attained, but it will happen of its own accord, if we will only let it."

From this poetic perspective, design can be seen as the shaping of spaces that allow the spontaneous to occur. Description never dulls experience if enough unplanned space is left around the plan. The ideas of regularity, of systems, of rules — these are always only limited human creations. That is not to embrace the radical relativity of the postmodernists, nor to imply that the future is utterly up for grabs, but to suggest that nature is stronger than we will ever be and *we cannot say anything certain about it.*

We go on hoping in vain for the pure and exact. But while waves in the ocean beat rhythmically on the shore, they never beat in the same rhythm. No two snowflakes are exactly the same. Alexander writes:

The character of nature is no mere poetic metaphor. It is a specific morphological character, a geometric character, which happens to be common to all those things in the world which are not man-made. Nature is never modular. Nature is full of almost similar units. We cannot even find two leaves which are the same.

Any rule or prescription is thus only an attempt at explaining the ineffable. When a design works, we can sense this at once. But the sensation is never planned. We love buildings in which we have fallen in love, or where the space looks out to the rest of the world to suggest that the whole has meaning. Despite all of our talk of ecological responsibility, space must be left for wonder and the preservation of the unknown.

Two photographs from Christian Norberg-Schultz's *Concept of Dwelling* illustrate this idea: On the left, a green, lush Norwegian forest. On the right, a dark wooden house with a solid thatched roof. Of course one belongs in the other. There is no jarring contrast, no doubt. This kind of building is not opposed to its landscape; its place in its surroundings suggests harmony. Martin Heidegger comes back again, with his most succinct advice for architects: "We dwell in that we build." Building only works when it instills us in the world. Dwelling means to belong to things you don't understand. The house is not a closed system, but one that opens toward the world.

Heidegger goes on to speak of "releasement," *Gelassenheit*, a word that he reinvigorates with meaning as he describes it as a letting go to the earth that allows nature to speak through you in your acts and structures. EXPO 2000 does not so much need to bring the world to Hannover as to show that Hannover already opens up toward the world. Visitors should be encouraged to see farther into the essence of their place, not through the imposition of blindly optimistic dreams, but through the beauty of the interconnected nature of our most important problems. We may ultimately be unequal to solving those problems, but opening to the world opens paths to understanding, and perhaps to the spark of intuition that leads to new solutions.

Heidegger points out that buildings should "bring the inhabited landscape close to humanity," rather than imposing humanity onto the landscape. The locally specific, traditional, or vernacular architecture has survived over the centuries because it accomplishes this. Norberg-Schultz speaks of the Einhaus of Lower Saxony, the large farmhouses on the North German plains built of "long ridges surrounded by groups of trees, looking like man-made hills which give structure to the surroundings." They make the landscape readable, but they do not pave it over with their intentions. Adolph Loos wrote in Austria in 1910 of the essentially biological nature of vernacular construction:

The peasant cuts out the spot on the green grass where the house is to be built and digs out the earth for the foundation walls. He makes the roof. What kind of roof? One that is beautiful or ugly? He does not know his aim was to build a house for himself, his family and his livestock and in this he has succeeded. Just as his neighbors and ancestors succeeded. As every animal which allows itself to be led by its instincts, succeeded.

A bit romantic, perhaps. But instinct does need to be combined with the latest in global ecological awareness. Can our awareness match the pace of the modern world? Kenneth Frampton writes that architecture must deal most poignantly with the present, instead of the past or the future:

> Building by virtue of its materiality and actuality cannot realize itself in terms of some redeeming future. For all its relative permanence it has no choice like most instrumental acts but to exist in its own historical moment. It has as its objective task the non-reductive realization of humanity here and now. Its true object is no longer the idealized projections of the Enlightenment but rather the physical constitution of the necessary attributes of place.

Among the biggest obstacles to a sustainable and releasing design is the question of time. Can anything be built quickly that is designed to last, be it a building, a city, a road, or even a poem or a story? Human works that endure are not concocted overnight, changing lead into gold. They need to balance the sudden flash of individual insight with the slow testing of the waters, so by the time they are built, used, and gently aged, no one person or idea can be identified as being solely responsible. Architecture belongs to no one. It expresses the essential anonymity of a species at one with its niche, as both are created together.

At times, design must defer to the insights of other disciplines. Town planners often imagine that they can legislate the behavior of those who live in the model worlds they have designed; they want the inhabitants of their towns to live out a planned dream. But the built environment can only do so much, and people have shown that they will not let infrastructure tell them what to do. Design should leave room for the flexible use of other builders of society. At its best, it can suggest new poetic, aesthetic, and scientific insights, rather than imagine it can provide all things.

World's Fairs and The Language of the Future

What is necessary is a framework by which innovators in different fields may be encouraged to build something more profound than the sum of its parts. We must leave room for the evolutionary play that comes from the chance encounter of different ideas. This is the consequence of the principle of humility, and an escape from the tyranny of the plan.

A useful historical antecedent may be the World's Columbian Exposition of 1893 in Chicago, which may be the most influential of previous world's fairs in terms of assessing a present and offering a model for its future. Almost nothing remains of the construction, but the image of the world put forth at the event contrasts starkly with the mainstream of American modernism that replaced it.

The World's Columbian Exposition was proposed to commemorate a date nearly as auspicious as the end of the millennium: the four-hundredth anniversary of Columbus's supposed discovery of America. The most celebrated designers of the United States were called upon to collaborate on the exposition's design. Frederick Law Olmstead chose the site on the shores of Lake Michigan. (It was a stretch of unreclaimed marshland that would justify instant protection today, but that was not in the nineteenth century's arena of concern.) He worked with architect Daniel Burnham, who later earned fame for his Flatiron Building in New York, to devise an overall plan as a miniature version of the American national landscape, combining the grid and the garden, linking park and city with wide landscaped boulevards. The idea was not to focus on industrial innovation as in previous fairs, but to present the artistic and cultural ambitions of a nation poised to take a leading role in the world.

New York architects Richard Morris Hunt and McKim, Mead, and White contributed buildings. From

Boston came Peabody & Stearns, and from Chicago, Louis Sullivan. Sculptor Auguste St.-Gaudens was the chief art consultant, and he commented on the gathering as "the greatest meeting of artists since the fifteenth century." It should be noted that they were all American artists. (Humility was not really an overriding concern of the exposition's designers, but it was true that no one person was in charge.)

The durability of the 1893 fair was specifically temporary, not sustainable. The building material was a mixture of jute, cement, and plaster, to emulate alabaster in structures that were meant to last only a summer. (Actually, such temporary intervention might in fact be more sustainable than the dream of creating a whole new city where there is little demand for one.) The style of the construction was an ornate classicism, which Robert Stern sees as an attempt to establish America as a great nation by virtue of a self-proclaimed role as guardian of the classical tradition. Louis Sullivan, however, came to see the classical monumentality of the site as an aberration that set back American functional modernism by fifty years.

The fair dealt with myriad readable symbols, which only a diverse group of cooperative thinkers could successfully interpret for a popular audience. There were allegories of Art, Science, Industry, and Agriculture, along with carnival rides and attractions. Twenty-seven million people visited the exposition in the single summer it was open. That was nearly one-third the population of the United States at the time. The nation was clearly impressed by the monumental classical vision of what a city could be, even though it did little to alleviate the strained conditions of the Chicago slums, which lie, then as now, just a few miles away from the site.

Architecturally, the pictures of the site show it as an impressive and unified place, and detailed study of the individual pieces reveals an organic sense that could only have been created by designers using a general guiding philosophy. Yet it remains a success of appearance, not permanence. What were its lasting, sustainable effects? Those who worked on the fair were asked to build major, lasting buildings in the same model. The Chicago waterfront parks were expanded, and the subsequent dredging of the Chicago River suggested to Burnham a future for Chicago in which it might resemble Paris — the urban center as artwork. These designers did not have enough political power to win wide acceptance for their vision, but they did have a measure of success in Washington, D.C., where they refurbished L'Enfant's plan for the capital city with a series of neo-Federalist buildings that stand to this day. The World's Columbian Exposition was like a cardboard model of the real project: It showed what a collaboration of brilliant designers might look like if they were given the encouragement to work together around a common aesthetic vision.

Another important antecedent is the Artists' Pavilion at the Osaka Exposition of 1970. This project was initiated by the organization E.A.T. (Experiments in Art and Technology), founded by engineer Billy Kluwer and artist Robert Rauschenberg in 1966. E.A.T. was founded to provide artists with the technical expertise to realize their ideas with the most up-to-date technology available. The pavilion was designed to show how art — in particular, art merged with technology — could comment on and contribute to the possibilities of the future. Kluwer explained: "Artists are not limited to functionality. They are sensitive to scale. They question assumptions, and assume responsibility for their creations. They make a strong statement with a minimum of means and a single-mindedness of purpose."

The Artist's Pavilion at Osaka was commissioned by PepsiCo to highlight the adventurous possibilities of new technologies. But the E.A.T. artists questioned the dominant mode of futuristic thinking. When the Exposition's planners demanded that the pavilion be a large geodesic-like dome in the tradition of monumental world's fair architecture at that time, the artists and engineers, finding that too banal, covered the dome with a constantly rising cloud of mist, cloaking the regularity of the imposed design with an organic, volcanic feel. Inside were mirrors, sounds and materials from all over the world, and telexes that allowed visitors to communicate internationally, all of which emphasized a diversity of possible cultures. Handheld radios, the Walkmans of the past, could be carried through the exhibit to pick up changing broadcasts from around the inside of the sphere. A cooperative effort of many thinkers and designers from all over the world, the Artist's Pavilion was one of the most popular attractions at the fair.

Still, the Osaka Expo did not stray too far from a fairly typical focus on the technology of tomorrow. The Hannover EXPO, on the other hand, is based on ideas of restraint, awareness, and concern for solving the world's problems, not hiding them behind a wall of promising machines. Now more than ever, cooperation is key. Drawing on the *spirit* of previous world's fairs, Hannover should call upon an international consortium of artists, designers and technologists to address tomorrow's challenges in ways no one person could engineer alone.

With EXPO 2000, we propose that the community of designers rally around a common ecological vision, with aesthetic direction open to choice. Cooperative design work may help to diminish the quirks of individual egos, generating the creative, comprehensive strategies that might never arise from the work of one.

We would like the *language* of sustainability, a still-evolving language, to be the framework for the design thinking that informs Hannover's vision for the next millennium. Christopher Alexander's ideas about group process can easily be extended to a large plan:

When a group of people try to do something together, they usually fail, because their assumptions are different at every stage. But with a common language, the assumptions should be explicit from the start. Of course they no longer have the medium of a single mind, as an individual person does. But instead, the group uses the site "out there in front of them" as the medium in which the design takes shape. People walk around, wave their arms, gradually build up a common picture as the plan takes its shape. ...It is for this reason that the site becomes so much more important for a group. The site speaks to the people—the building forms itself—and people experience it as something received, not created.

For successful cooperation to be the hallmark of Hannover, those involved will need to have some agreement that sustainability is an important goal, as well as a commitment to understanding the ramifications of their design work well beyond the immediate context. The ecological integrity of materials, the effect of the Expo on the overall landscape, the project's role in meeting the basic needs of visitors and inhabitants now and in the future, and the articulation of an affirming and optimistic vision for the next millennium can all be addressed in a cooperative spirit.

EXPO 2000 is like an imaginary city that must be built as something real and enduring to prove its point.

As author Italo Calvino alludes: "Cities, like dreams, are made of desires and fears. Even if the thread of their discourse is secret, or their rules absurd…everything conceals something else." The ecologically sustainable vision for Hannover on the cusp of the millennium is motivated by the fear of a devastated planet and a desire to show that we have a real chance to save it and continue the evolution of our species. There are no easy rules to follow, and every choice not only hides another but suggests a new thread of inquiry. The full exploration of this interwoven net of questions, desires and fears is the sane path toward an ecological resolution of the fate of this earth.

AFTERWORD: CAN DESIGN SAVE THE WORLD?

THE HANNOVER PRINCIPLES, SUSTAINABILITY, AND A DECADE OF INTELLIGENT DESIGN

David Rothenberg

I was honored to be invited by Bill McDonough to join the team writing *The Hannover Principles* in his New York office in the spring of 1992. I had been working with Norwegian philosopher Arne Naess on articulating the tenets of deep ecology, a school of environmental thinking that uses philosophy to ferret out the conceptual roots of our relationship with nature. Deep ecology is based on a platform of eight points, similar in form to the Hannover Principles, and for several years I had been trying to get Naess to clarify his platform to make it more consistent and clear. Bill saw the relevance of this experience to the document he was trying to produce, and so we worked together trying to gather and synthesize a wealth of well-intentioned, principled perspectives on the design of the human world into a document with rigor and applicable power. As we prepared a vision for Hannover's Exposition for the millennium, we drew from the highlights of previous World's Fairs and the wise words of thinkers like Marshall McLuhan, Lewis Mumford, and even Italo

Calvino, who knew that design was made out of desires and fears.

Even though Expo 2000 was not the celebration of sustainability that we hoped it would be, the Hannover Principles turned out to be tremendously important, inspiring thousands to recognize that design can be at the heart of constructive efforts to remake human life into something that can enhance the planet instead of using it up. Not only have the Principles shaped the work of William McDonough + Partners, McDonough Braungart Design Chemistry and all of their many clients, they have become a framework for action and decision-making for other values-based institutions as well. At Yale University, for example, the Principles helped inspire the Yale School of Forestry and Environmental Studies to initiate a joint program on environment and design with the Yale School of Architecture.

This renewal of the connection between design and the environment is a key legacy of the Hannover Principles. Environmentalism as a movement has often appeared inherently pessimistic, built upon quite justifiable alarm at the tragic consequences of what are usually called progress and prosperity: exhaustion of nonrenewable resources, overpopulation, overproduction, global monoculture, mass extinction, destruction of valuable ecosystems, and rapid climate change. All these things are real and present dangers.

But principled design offers an alternative, a fundamental optimism and the renewed possibility of taking pride in the things we make. Problems can and must be solved. We can build better products, better manufacturing processes, better buildings, and thus a better way of planning and making our world. Design, then, is fundamentally solution oriented, and by its very nature is hopeful and constructive.

Yet many people still think design is more about appearance than structure. Others see an opposition between ecologically intelligent design and prosperous commerce. The beauty of the Hannover Principles is that they provide a framework for resolving those conflicts. As Bill and Michael have applied the Principles to their firms' work over the past decade, they have moved design beyond mere aesthetics toward the re-visioning of the human-made products that fill up our world. And as WM+P and MBDC work with their clients—Ford, Nike, Herman Miller, The City of Chicago among them—they have brilliantly shown that intelligent design is not only environmentally sound but profitable as well. Decision-makers listen to their ideas.

Bill always told me that if you want to influence a company, you must start at the top. Go straight to the CEO, and rather than telling him what he wants to hear, tell him what he needs to hear — that sustainability, interdependence, and eco-effectiveness are not sentences from the judge of industrial capitalism, but essential opportunities that any business who wants to be a leader in this new millennium must follow.

The Hannover Principles are useful in this ongoing conversation with business leaders because they are not axioms of resistance, but keys for success in an enlightened future in which we accept the damage we have done and recognize the need for change.

The most clearly pragmatic message is probably number five: Create safe objects of long-term value. Really, what else would be worth devoting one's life to making? Anything less would be dangerous or shoddy, and who wants to be identified with making anything like that? Unfortunately, too many people are motivated mainly by the opportunity for short-term profits, and that's why this principle is worth taking to heart — and why it is heartening to see that many leaders are doing just that.

The Principles are not just easy moralism, nine "you shoulds" that people will read and nod their heads to and then politely ignore. This is serious business. Principle six, "Eliminate the concept of waste," is probably the most radical idea here, because it involves completely rethinking the way resources are extracted, used, and thrown away. In *Cradle to Cradle*, McDonough and Braungart wisely point out that in the natural world, one creature's waste is another's food. Learning from nature, we can see that the waste generated by industry must become clean enough to eat. When that idea moves from the realm of science fiction into reality, then we can honestly say that we have figured out how to build truly advanced technology. Some readers might find such an idea to be hopelessly utopian, but design is the art of realizing and engineering the impossible, and if we do not set lofty goals, we will never achieve innovation or lasting greatness.

The Principles also recognize that we can only get better by openly sharing knowledge. Success in business has previously depended on competition and jealous guarding of trade secrets. That is no way to save the world. No one will be able to copyright the next industrial revolution. Increasing market share will have to arise from genuine innovation, cutting-edge thinking and tools that push a company's activities closer to the eco-effective and sustainable dream.

The value of humility informs the Principles too: We are asked to consider the limits of design. Alone, design cannot save the world — there is only so much a new technology or a new approach to making things can change the way people think and behave. Writers of manifestos have been known over the years for getting carried away, or letting others get carried away, by confusing a call to action with a book of rigid rules. Taking the lessons of the past to heart, McDonough and Braungart have never made the mistake of letting their ideas become frozen in ideology. They have been the most effective communicators of the movement to reconnect design with environmentalism because they do not simply denounce the status quo; they help their clients discover principled solutions that honor a wide spectrum of perspectives.

Because design creates the visible human world, it has a lot to answer for. Our contemporary built environment is often ugly, ostentatious, inefficient and disheartening — perhaps a mirror of our fragmented minds and souls. The things we use everyday in our homes and workplaces are often not good for us. But there is a better way, and WM+P and MBDC have been hashing out a new path for a decade now. They have been able to stay the course because they are guided by the Hannover Principles. Over the last ten years, as the meaning of sustainability has grown diffuse to the point of being meaningless, the Principles have provided a reliable design framework. As sustainable growth has come to mean the level of expansion a company can sustain without collapsing, the Principles remind designers that sustainability is rooted in more enduring values: the cycles of the natural world, the eternal interdependence of living things, the rights of humanity and nature to co-exist.

Sustainability is so much easier to co-opt as a marketing slogan than it is to put into practice because taking it seriously involves a philosophical about-face in the very way we do business. It asks for transformations and dares us to choose courses of action that more often than not sound like unreachable dreams. But dreams can be made real, and making them real should be based on principles, not on hot air. I am glad to see that the Hannover Principles have proved worthy of the task. Ten years after their original publication they are still bringing dreams to fruition and I expect they will be guiding us for many years to come.

BIBLIOGRAPHY

Alexander, Christopher, *The Timeless Way of Building*, New York: Oxford University Press, 1979.

Arendt, Hannah, *The Human Condition*, Chicago: University of Chicago Press, 1958.

Beatley, Timothy, *Green Urbanism*, Washington D.C.: Island Press, 2000.

Berman, Marshall, *All That Is Solid Melts into Air: The Experience of Modernity*, New York: Viking Penguin, 1982.

Boardman, Philip, *The Worlds of Patrick Geddes*, London: Routledge and Kegan Paul, 1978.

Borgmann, Albert, *Technology and the Character of Contemporary Life*, Chicago: University of Chicago Press, 1984.

Brown, Lester, *Building a Sustainable Society*, New York: W.W. Norton, 1981.

Brown, Lester, *et al.*, *State of the World 1992*, New York: W.W. Norton, 1992.

Brown, Lester, *et al.*, *State of the World 2000*, New York: W.W. Norton, 2000.

Brown, Lester, Christopher Flavin, and Sandra Postel, *Saving the Planet*, New York: W.W. Norton, 1991.

Calvino, Italo, *Invisible Cities*, New York: Harcourt Brace Jovanovich, 1974.

Canetti, Elias, *Crowds and Power*, trans. Carl Stewart, New York: Farrar, Straus, & Giroux, 1984.

Carr, Marilyn, ed. *The Appropriate Technology Reader*, London: Intermediate Technology Publications, 1985.

Carson, Rachel, *Silent Spring*, Boston: Houghton Mifflin, 1994.

Collingwood, R.G. *The Idea of Nature*, Oxford: Clarendon Press, 1945.

Cronon, William, *Changes in the Land*, New York: Farrar, Straus & Giroux, 1983.

———, *Nature's Metropolis*, New York: W.W. Norton, 1991.

Daly, Herman, *Steady-State Economics*, Washington D.C.: Island Press, 1991.

Dessauer, Friedrich, "Technology In its Proper Sphere," in *Philosophy and Technology*, ed. Carl Mitcham and Robert Mackey, New York: Free Press, 1972.

Dewey, John, *Experience and Nature*, La Salle, Ill.: Open Court, 1929.

Diamond, Jared, *Guns, Germs, and Steel*, New York: W.W. Norton, 1999.

Dickson, David, *Alternative Technology and the Politics of Technical Change*, London: Fontana, 1974.

Dijksterhuis, E.J., *The Mechanization of the World Picture*, Oxford: Oxford University Press, 1961.

Dunn, P.D., *Appropriate Technology: Technology with a Human Face*, London: Macmillan, 1978.

Durrell, Lee, GAIA *State of the Ark Atlas*, New York: Doubleday, 1986.

Ehrenfeld, David, *The Arrogance of Humanism*, New York: Oxford University Press, 1978.

Elgin, Duane, *Voluntary Simplicity*, New York: William Morrow, 1981.

Ellul, Jacques, *The Technological Society*, New York: Knopf, 1965.

Enzensberger, Hans Magnus, *The Consciousness Industry: On Literature, Politics, and the Media*, New York: Seabury Press, 1974.

Fathy, Hassan, *Architecture for the Poor*, Chicago: University of Chicago Press, 1973.

———, *Natural Energy and Vernacular Architecture*, Chicago: University of Chicago Press, 1986.

Flavin, Christopher, *Energy and Architecture: The Solar and Conservation Potential*, Washington D.C.: Worldwatch Institute, 1986.

Flavin, Christopher, *et al.*, *Vital Signs 2002*, New York: W.W. Norton, 2002.

Flannery, Tim, *The Eternal Frontier,* New York: Grove Press, 2001.

Frampton, Kenneth, *Modern Architecture and the Critical Present*, London: AD Magazine, 1982.

Giedion, Siegfried, *Mechanization Takes Command: A Contribution to Anonymous History*, New York: Oxford University Press, 1948.

Gille, Bernard, *et al.*, *The History of Techniques*, New York: Gordon & Breach Scientific Publishers, 1986.

Hardison, O.B. Jr., *Disappearing through the Skylight: Culture and Technology in the 20th Century*, New York: Viking Penguin, 1989.

Heidegger, Martin, *Poetry, Language, Thought*, trans. Albert Hofstadter, New York: Harper & Row, 1971.

——, "The Question Concerning Technology," in *The Question Concerning Technology and other Essays*, tr. William Lovett, New York: Harper & Row, 1977.

Hough, M., *City Form and Natural Process*, London: Routledge, 1984.

Illich, Ivan, *Tools for Conviviality*, New York: Harper and Row, 1973.

Jacobs, Jane, *The Death and Life of Great American Cities*, New York: Vintage, 1992.

——, *Systems of Survival*, New York: Vintage, 1994.

Jonas, Hans, *The Imperative of Responsibility*, Chicago: University of Chicago Press, 1984.

Klee, Paul, *The Thinking Eye*, London: Lund Humphrey, 1961.

Krier, Rob, *Urban Space*, New York: Rizzoli, 1979.

Kval, Sigmund, "Complexity and Time: Breaking the Pyramid's Reign," in *Wisdom in the Open Air*, eds., Peter Reed and David Rothenberg, Minneapolis: University of Minnesota Press, 1992.

Lovejoy, A.J., "Nature as Aesthetic Norm," in *Modern Language Notes*, 42, no. 7, 1927, pp. 444–50.

Luhmann, Niklas, *Ecological Communication*, Chicago: University of Chicago Press, 1990.

Lyle, John Tillman, *Regenerative Design for Sustainable Development*, Hoboken: John Wiley & Sons, 1996.

Lyman, Francesca, *et al.*, *The Greenhouse Trap: What We're Doing to the Atmosphere and How We Can Slow Global Warming*, Boston: Beacon Press, 1990.

Marx, Leo, *The Machine in the Garden*, New York: Oxford University Press, 1964.

Maser, Chris, *The Redesigned Forest*, San Pedro, Calif: R & E Miles, 1988.

McHarg, Ian, *Design with Nature*, New York: Natural History Press, 1969.

McKibben, Bill, *The End of Nature*, New York: Random House, 1989.

McLuhan, Marshall, *Understanding Media: The Extensions of Man*, New York: McGraw Hill, 1964.

Meyrowitz, Joshua, *No Sense of Place: The Impact of Electronic Media on Social Behavior*, New York: Oxford University Press, 1985.

Morris, William, *News from Nowhere*, London: Routledge & Kegan Paul, 1970.

Mumford, Lewis, *Technics and Civilization*, New York: Harcourt, Brace Jovanovich, 1934.

———, *The Myth of the Machine*, New York: Harcourt, Brace and World, 1967.

Naess, Arne, with David Rothenberg, *Ecology, Community, and Lifestyle*, Cambridge University Press, 1989.

Nash, Roderick, *The Rights of Nature*, Madison: University of Wisconsin Press, 1989.

National Academy of Sciences, *One Earth, One Future*, Washington D.C.: National Academy Press, 1990.

Norberg-Schultz, Christian, *The Concept of Dwelling*, New York: Rizzoli, 1985.

Oelschlaeger, Max, *The Idea of Wilderness*, New Haven: Yale University Press, 1991.

Orr, David, *Earth in Mind*, Washington D.C.: Island Press, 1994.

———, *Ecological Literacy*, Albany: State University of New York Press, 1992.

Ortega y Gasset, José, "Thoughts on Technology," in *Philosophy and Technology*, Carl Mitcham and Robert Mackey, eds. New York: Free Press, 1972.

Papanek, Victor, *Design for the Real World: Human Ecology and Social Change*, Chicago: Academy Chicago Publishers, 1985.

Ramphal, Shridath, *Our Country, the Planet*, Washington D.C.: Island Press, 1992.

Renner, Michael, *Rethinking the Role of the Automobile*, Worldwatch Paper no. 84, Washington D.C.: Worldwatch Institute, 1988.

Ricketts, Taylor H., Eric Dinerstein, David M. Olsen, Colby J. Loucks, *et al.*, *Terrestrial Ecoregions of North America*, Washington D.C.: Island Press 1999.

Romanyshyn, Robert, *Technology as Symptom and Dream*, London: Routledge, 1990.

Rudovsky, Bernard, *Architecture without Architects*, New York: Doubleday, 1964.

Rybczynski, Witold, *Paper Heroes: A Review of Appropriate Technology*, New York: Doubleday, 1980.

Salem, Osama Shible, "Toward Sustainable Architecture and Urban Design: Categories, Methodologies, and Models," unpublished manuscript, Rensselaer Polytechnic Institute, 1990.

Schadewaldt, Wolfgang, "The Concepts of Nature and Technique According to the Greeks," in *Research in Philosophy and Technology*, 2, 1979, pp. 159-171.

Schell, Jonathan, *The Fate of the Earth*, New York: Alfred A. Knopf, 1982.

Schiller, Friedrich, *On the Aesthetic Education of Man*, trans. Reginald Snell, New York: Frederick Ungar, 1954.

Schumacher, E.F., *Small is Beautiful: Economics as if People Mattered*, New York: Harper Torchbooks, 1973.

Schurman, Egbert, *Technology and the Future: A Philosophical Challenge*, trans. Herbert D. Morton, Toronto: Wedge Publishing Foundation, 1980.

Society of Environmental Toxicology and Chemistry, *A Technical Framework for Life-Cycle Assessments*, Washington D.C.: SETAC, 1991.

Steinberg, Ted, *Down to Earth*, Oxford, UK: Oxford University Press, 2002.

Taylor, John, *Commonsense Architecture*, New York: Norton, 1983.

Taylor, Peter, *Respect for Nature*, Princeton: Princeton University Press, 1986.

Todd, Nancy Jack, and John Todd, *Bioshelters, Ocean Arks, City Farming: Ecology as the Basis of Design*, San Francisco: Sierra Club Books, 1984.

——, *From Eco-Cities to Living Machines*, Berkeley: North Atlantic Books, 1994.

Turner, John, *Housing by People: Toward Autonomy in Building Environments*, New York: Pantheon, 1977.

Van der Ryn, Sim, and Peter Calthorpe, *Sustainable Communities*, San Francisco: Sierra Club Books, 1986.

von Weizscker, Carl Friedrich, *The Unity of Nature*, New York: Farrar, Straus, & Giroux, 1980.

Wells, Malcolm, *Gentle Architecture*, New York: McGraw Hill, 1981.

Wilson, Alexander, *The Culture of Nature*, Cambridge: Blackwell, 1992.

Wilson, Edward O., *Biophilia*, Cambridge, Mass: Harvard University Press, 1986.

————, *The Future of Life*, New York: Alfred A. Knopf, 2002.

Winner, Langdon, *Autonomous Technology: Technics-out-of-Control as a Theme in Political Thought*, Cambridge: MIT Press, 1977.

Winner, Langdon, *The Whale and the Reactor: A Search for Limits in an Age of High Technology*, Chicago: University of Chicago Press, 1986.

World Commission on Environment and Development, *Our Common Future*, London: Oxford University Press, 1987.

World Resources Institute, *Environmental Almanac*, Boston: Houghton Mifflin, 1992.

Worster, Donald, *Nature's Economy*, Cambridge, UK: Cambridge University Press, 1994.

Zimmerli, Walther, "Variety in Technology, Unity in Responsibility?" in *Technology and Contemporary Life*, ed. Paul Durbin, Boston: D. Reidel, 1988.

CONTRIBUTORS

TERESA HEINZ KERRY has long been recognized as one of the nation's premier environmental leaders. She is chairman of the Heinz Family Philanthropies and of the Howard Heinz Endowment, where she directed the creation and design of a grantmaking program supporting the environment. The creator of the prestigious Heinz Awards, an annual program recognizing outstanding vision and achievement in five areas including the environment, she also helped create the H. John Heinz III Center for Science, Economics and the Environment, a unique attempt to bring together representatives of business, government, the scientific community and environmental groups to collaborate on the development of mutually acceptable yet scientifically sound environmental policies. She is Vice Chair of Environmental Defense and was one of ten representatives from non-governmental organizations attached to the U.S. Delegation to the U.N. Conference on Environment and Development (Earth Summit) in Brazil in 1992. A co-founder and board member of the Alliance to End Childhood Lead Poisoning, she has endowed a professorship in environmental management at the Harvard Business School and a chair in environmental policy at Harvard's John F. Kennedy School of Government, and since 1995 she has sponsored annual conferences designed to inform women about the relationship of health and environmental issues to their daily lives. She is married to U.S. Senator John Kerry.

MICHAEL BRAUNGART is a chemist, the founder of the Environmental Protection Encouragement Agency (EPEA) in Hamburg, Germany, and co-founder and principal of McDonough Braungart Design Chemistry. Prior to starting EPEA, he was the director of the chemistry for Greenpeace. Since 1984 he has been lecturing at universities, businesses, and institutions around the world on ecological chemistry and material flows management. Dr. Braungart is the recipient of numerous honors, awards and fellowships from the Heinz Foundation, the W. Alton Jones Foundation, and other organizations. With William McDonough, he is the co-author of *Cradle to Cradle: Remaking the Way We Make Things*, published in 2002 by North Point Press.

WILLIAM MCDONOUGH is an architect and the founding principal of William McDonough + Partners, Architecture and Community Design, and McDonough Braungart Design Chemistry, both based in Charlottesville, Virginia. From 1994 to 1999 he served as dean of the school of architecture at the University of Virginia. In 1999 *Time* magazine selected him as a "Hero for the Planet," stating that "his utopianism is grounded in a unified philosophy that—in demonstrable and practical ways—is changing the design of the world." In 1996 he received the Presidential Award for

Sustainable Development, the highest environmental honor given in the United States.

DAVID ROTHENBERG is an associate professor of philosophy at the New Jersey Institute of Technology. He is the founding editor of the journal *Terra Nova: Nature and Culture* and editor of the *Terra Nova* book series. His essays have appeared in *Parabola*, *The Nation*, and *Wired*, among other publications, and he is the author of *Sudden Music*, *Always the Mountains* and *Hand's End: Technology and the Limits of Nature*, in which a version of "The Meaning of Sustainablity" was reprinted.

CHRIS REITER, the editor of the tenth anniversary edition of *The Hannover Principles*, is an editorial consultant to McDonough Braungart Design Chemistry, William McDonough + Partners and a variety of arts and environmental organizations, including The Biodiversity Project, The Wildlands Project and BirdBrain Dance. He is the founding editor of Blue Ridge Press, a syndicated column service distributing environmental commentary to Southern newspapers. His writing on nature and culture has appeared in *Natural History*, *Wild Earth* and *Rhythm Music*, among many other publications.

ENVIRONMENTAL PROTECTION ENCOURAGEMENT AGENCY is a scientific consultancy working with companies from a variety of industries on improving product quality, utility and environmental performance through eco-effectiveness. A design strategy developed by Braungart and McDonough, eco-effectiveness integrates chemistry, biology, environmental engineering and design to develop consumer-friendly, biocompatible products that also generate shareholder value. EPEA's clients include Ben & Jerry's, BASF, Ecover, Guilford and Novartis.

MCDONOUGH BRAUNGART DESIGN CHEMISTRY is a product and process design firm working with client companies such as BASF, Nike, Herman Miller, Shaw Inc, Visteon and Ford Motor Company to develop design strategies that generate ecological, economic and social value. MBDC's Design Protocol is a science-based process that maximizes the utility and value of material assets while creating safe, healthful products. Founded by McDonough and Braungart in 1995, MBDC is now at the forefront of the emerging movement of designers and business leaders dedicated to creating high-quality materials that provide nourishment for nature after their useful lives or circulate through industrial systems in endless cycles of production, recovery and reuse.

WILLIAM MCDONOUGH + PARTNERS is an architecture and community design firm practicing a positive, principled approach to design. The firm's designs support the creation of community within an ecologically intelligent framework. Studies of each project's context lead to an "essay of clues" that responds to the physical, cultural and climactic setting as well the client's unique needs, culture and goals. By considering a diverse range of economic, ecological and cultural criteria and by pursuing quality at all scales, WM+P taps positive strategies of change to encourage patterns of human activity and settlement that are restorative and regenerative by design.